Magical Mystical Poems

Carol Mays

ISBN Number:
9798726154053

Published in West Brookfield, Massachusetts

Cover photo by egal/Bigstock.com

To my husband, Gary Blanchard, who inspires my life
and my work in so many ways.

Table of Contents

Introduction

What if the basis of "reality" is not the man-made matrix into which we structure our days and hours? What if it's not the outlines and the patterns by which we sort and compartmentalize our lives? Perhaps all those configurations are just accumulated cultural habits that may or may not have outlived their purpose.

You may have noticed that when people refer to "the real world," they are referring to something negative— perhaps the unforgiving push-and-pull of daily life or the disillusioning process of rubbing up against roadblocks.

At times we long for something more—something that seems more intrinsic, soulful, exciting, meaningful, flexible, and promising. We long to transcend (or to get beneath) the presets, to an unvarnished world of possibilities, where we can see the magic and the mysteries of life with fresh eyes. We want to feel innate potential and power and open up again to expansive feelings and dreams, to our true humanity.

Although all things "magical" and "mystical" are often sidelined in our culture as relatively insignificant, to me these words speak to the very heart of reality. Even on a physical level, quantum mechanics has found that in an apparent vacuum, particles mysteriously pop in and out of existence. On a spiritual level, we all know that life would be quite stale and meaningless without the little sweet mysteries and surprises that sustain us and remind us of a wider, deeper worldview. The aim of this book is to feed our souls not so much by escaping from "reality" as by remembering reality—one that we are privileged to be a part of and that is wider and deeper than anything we can imagine.

Throughout my life, I have been collecting images that struck me as magical. I have written and/or compiled books on subjects as divergent as the sea, Halloween, and faith. Most have included poems by myself and other writers. I have reprinted many of these poems here, along with others that have not yet been published. At first I thought I would partition this book into "magical poems" and "mystical poems," but as I worked on it, I realized that all the poems are on a continuum between the two, and many would be difficult to categorize separately.

I have been inspired by putting these pages together. Here's hoping that you will find something that nurtures your soul as well.

I

Nature's
Enchantments

A Woodland Walk

The pensiveness of the sky
 is broken by the cry of a crow,
 by trees distilling intimacy
 and moist, vibrant expectancy.
 Violets, ferns, and birches
 share life-giving vapors.
 The chalk-bleak horizon
 and pungent, poignant odors
 whisper sonorous secrets.
 The visitor is enveloped
 in this pithy, soulful world,
 all cells saturated
 with a suggestive sustenance.

-- Carol Mays

Rain on the Hill
(from the first stanza)

. . . From the ancient firs
Aroma of balsam drifts,
And the silent places are filled
With elusive odors distilled . . .

-- Lucy Maud Montgomery

To a Cedar

I had nearly forgotten who I was
Until I sensed your easy strength
    and heard the timelessness
    of your years;
Until I caught the sparkle
    of your lacy light
    and showered in your fragrance
Until I recognized your verdancy
    jumping the primal circuit.

                -- Carol Mays

A Day Off

Let us put awhile away
All the cares of work-a-day,
For a golden time forget,
Task and worry, toil and fret,
Let us take a day to dream
In the meadow by the stream. . .

Where the wild-wood whisper stirs
We may talk with lisping firs,
We may gather honeyed blooms
In the dappled forest glooms,
We may eat of berries red
O'er the emerald upland spread.

We may linger as we will
In the sunset valleys still,
Till the gypsy shadows creep
From the starlit land of sleep,
And the mist of evening gray
Girdles round our pilgrim way.

We may bring to work again
Courage from the tasselled glen,
Bring a strength unfailing won
From the paths of cloud and sun,
And the wholesome zest that springs
From all happy, growing things.
                -- Lucy Maud Montgomery

Moonlit Night

It seemed as though the heavens
had kissed the earth to silence,
so that, amid glistening flowers,
she must now dream heavenly dreams.

The breeze passed through the fields;
the corn stirred softly;
the forest rustled lightly,
so clear and starry was the night.

And my soul spread
wide its wings;
took flight through the silent land
as though it were flying home.

       -- Joseph Eichendorff
     -- Translated by Philip Miller

Pandora's Songs

. . . As an immortal nightingale
I sing behind the summer sky
Thro' leaves of starlight gold and pale
That shiver with my melody,
Along the wake of the full-moon
Far on to oceans, and beyond
Where the horizons vanish down
In darkness clear as diamond. . .

-- Trumbull Stickney

Hymn to the Night

I heard the trailing garments of the Night
Sweep through her marble halls!
I saw her sable skirts all fringed with light
From the celestial walls!

I felt her presence, by its spell of might,
Stoop o'er me from above;
The calm, majestic presence of the Night,
As of the one I love.

I heard the sounds of sorrow and delight,
The manifold, soft chimes,
That fill the haunted chambers of the Night,
Like some old poet's rhymes.

From the cool cisterns of the midnight air
My spirit drank repose;
The fountain of perpetual peace flows there,—
From those deep cisterns flows.

O holy Night! from thee I learn to bear
What man has borne before!
Thou layest thy finger on the lips of Care,
And they complain no more.

Peace! Peace! Orestes-like I breathe this
   prayer!
Descend with broad-winged flight,

The welcome, the thrice-prayed for, the most
    fair,
The best-beloved Night!

    -- Henry Wadsworth Longfellow

Luminous Visitor

Out a dark window
my cat and I search for eyes.
There—two flashing pink!

-- Carol Mays

To See a World
(from *Auguries of Innocence*)

To see a World in a Grain of Sand
And a Heaven in a Wild Flower,
Hold Infinity in the palm of your hand
And Eternity in an hour.

-- William Blake

The Wheel in September

I've startled a frog, who leaps in flashes.
He and a grasshopper zigzag away.
The lawn whispers mildly, in tune with the sun,
Yet something's amiss--the air is unsettled.
Squirrels and I stash away seeds,
salvaged from spent, rain-ravaged beds.
Bees are now torpid and cling to the mums.
Bedraggled zinnias give up the ghost.

What becomes of the Grim Reaper's harvest,
of creatures who cannot withstand the strain?
The mystery hides in an infinite point—
the one in the center of The Great Hub—
the crux of a myriad transformations.

-- Carol Mays

Sitting at Night on the Moon Viewing Terrace

This autumn the days have been hot
but each evening cool weather returns.
The last few nights I have sat outside
until the water clock struck the third watch.

Brisk wind, stars glittering and fading;
floating clouds, welcomed and seen off by the
  moon.
When I pursue happiness I can never find it;
now happiness has come of itself.

-- Yang Wan-li
-- Translated by Jonathan Chaves

A Vagabond Song

There is something in the autumn that is
  native to my blood—
Touch of manner, hint of mood;
And my heart is like a rhyme,
With the yellow and the purple and the
  crimson keeping time.

The scarlet of the maples can shake me like
  a cry
Of bugles going by.
And my lonely spirit thrills
To see the frosty asters like a smoke upon
  the hills.

There is something in October sets the
  gypsy blood astir;
We must rise and follow her,
When from every hill of flame
She calls and calls each vagabond by
  name.

-- Bliss Carman

October-November

Indian-summer-sun
With crimson feathers whips away the mists;
Dives through the filter of trellises
And gilds the silver on the blotched arbor-seats.

Now gold and purple scintillate
On trees that seem dancing
In delirium;
Then the moon
In a mad orange flare
Floods the grape-hung night.

                  -- Hart Crane

November Sky

Stark, leafless branches
against a steel-blue sky,
hauntingly alive.

-- Carol Mays

Velvet Shoes

Let us walk in the white snow
In a soundless space;
With footsteps quiet and slow,
At a tranquil pace,
Under veils of white lace.

I shall go shod in silk,
And you in wool,
White as a white cow's milk,
More beautiful
Than the breast of a gull.

We shall walk through the still town
In a windless peace;
We shall step upon white down,
Upon silver fleece,
Upon softer than these.

We shall walk in velvet shoes:
Wherever we go
Silence will fall like dews
On white silence below.
We shall walk in the snow.

-- Elinor Wylie

After the Ice Storm

In the bright sunlight
one drop sparkled copper-red—
magical melting.

-- Carol Mays

November Rabbit

Vanishing mid-chomp,
kicking up a fluff of snow,
spooked somehow away.

    -- Carol Mays

A Shoveler's Reward

Under the full moon
fallen snow has stretched the sky,
bathing me in white.

-- Carol Mays

February Twilight

I stood beside a hill
Smooth with new-laid snow,
A single star looked out
From the cold evening glow.

There was no other creature
That saw what I could see—
I stood and watched the evening star
As long as it watched me.

-- Sara Teasdale

II

Mystical Mysteries

True Life

We ease into it—
the larger life surrounding
our self-direction.

From birds and crickets
and more we are distracted
by things that steal time.

Again we find home
in this pulsating life flow
within and without.

-- Carol Mays

Your Eyes

No finer jewels exist on earth
Than your sparkling eyes to me.
Like mirrors set in an infinite row,
Displaying your hopes, thoughts,
   fears, and joys,
They reveal all hopes, thoughts,
   fears, and joys,
Reflecting lights and skies and oceans,
Portals to space, time, and humanity—
To all that really matters.

-- Carol Mays

Heart of the Sun
(song lyrics)

Images of ages past
coming out of the light—
in my heart
I know the light has come
from the heart of the sun.

Time is a steady flow,
takes us along with it as it goes.
Time has brought us to this place,
filled our longing with a state of grace.
The light that shines is the light of life,
shining out from the soul
The yin and yang—
two hearts beat as one
in the heart of the sun.

Fire and water,
the yang and the yin—
opposites blending, a new life begins,
open and willing to let the light in.

Images of ages past
coming out of the light—
in my heart
I know that you have come
from the heart of the sun.

-- Gary Blanchard

Two Hearts

Two hearts were called,
Amidst the cacophony of life,
Amidst the fruitfulness of life.
Evolving from timelessness,
Moving in the center of existence.

Now each finds in the calling,
Beyond the restrictions of space,
An ever more central reality,
An ever more expanding reality,
Sensing even through dissonance,
Home, in its ever-pulsing joy.

-- Carol Mays

Hands of Time

(song lyrics)

Floating in the wonderland of dreams,
I see the sky below my feet.
Soaring through the world, I see the scenes
Of people living in the world below.
Looking at them, I can see the tears.
And all the hope that lies beneath the fears.

All around me I can hear the sounds
Of nature as she wakens from her sleep.
And behind me I can see the years
That poured around me as I lived my life.
And I surrender to the light
And offer myself to the loving hands;
The hands of time.

-- Gary Blanchard

Peace Like a River
(song lyrics)

Down through the ages, the river has run;
The river will run evermore.
Through all of life's stages, the river moves
   on;
Flowing to life's golden shore.

Peace like a river flows through my heart,
Opening love's golden gate.
Bringing together those broken apart,
Reaching to those who await.

Peace like a river runs through my soul,
Flowing from morning 'till night,
Causing the broken ones to be whole,
Turning the darkness to light.

Peace like a river runs through the world;
The river brings healing and light.
It flows like a banner that's boldly unfurled;
Let it engulf us tonight.

Down through the ages the river has run;
The river will run evermore.
Through all of life's stages the river moves
   on;
Flowing to life's golden shore.

--Gary Blanchard

Organic Whole

Our sweet connection to
sun-lit forsythias,
leaping squirrels, and
chirping chickadees—
deeper than a lifespan,
closer than a heartbeat.

-- Carol Mays

To a Wild Witch

With flowing robes,
pungent herbs,
arching doors,
organic walls,
and eerie lights,
you take on trappings
of one thought evil.
Yet in you beats
an open heart—
one always skirting
curdled customs,
sterile allegiances,
trivial tyrannies—
one ever seeking
reunions with roots,
transforming spaces,
raw possibilities.

      -- Carol Mays

At Perception's Edge
    (song lyrics)

At perception's edge
I see a holy light.
From the gentle glow,
the truth is burning bright.
Love is taking flight,
flying into night.

At perception's edge,
the song is in the heart.
The veil of doubt and fear
is slowly blown apart.
I feel a knowledge start
to open up the heart.

At perception's edge
the soul can truly see
the origins of life
that bind humanity.
Love is the key
that sets the spirit free.

At perception's edge
I see a holy light . . .

        -- Gary Blanchard

October 15, 1991

Scattered images flicker,
    as an evening passes:
Leaves riding the rain,
    in a bittersweet farewell;
A singer's warmth beamed
    to thousands of vehicles;
Ghosts swinging from strings
    in a Halloween display;
Sakharov's casket carried
    in a documentary;
A boy brimming with youth,
    delivering news on
A Union birthing nations,
    eight thousand miles away.

To work-weary eyes,
    strained and myopic,
Just routine impressions
    of another hectic day.
But these are the pulses
    of the unfolding cosmos,
The eddies and streams of
    forces and formations.
Being a mere ripple
    in this dazzling array
Is to be soaked to the core
    with a quintessential gift.
                    -- Carol Mays

A Secret World

Along a country road,
beyond the guard rail,
past the visible vines,
lurks an ancient jungle.
Most who travel pass
don't have an inkling of
the depth of the danger—
this cliff so close by,
this mystery in their midst.

The steep-slanting ground
and lush vegetation
in quintessential green
drop, and drop again
to a long-forgotten brook
that one can only hear—
though perhaps by peering,
one can glimpse some sunlight
sparkling from its surface.

After blithely flowing
through this lost world
of twisted roots and tree trunks,
the creek quickly merges
with the Quaboag River,
and, coming into normalcy,
loses some allure.

Another mystery calls from
this roughly hewn valley
(gouged out by ice sheets
and still too severe
for human encroachment).
More resonant than the birds
and deeper than the stream,
it registers in a region
somewhere in the soul.

Taking one by surprise,
this precarious paradise
suddenly feels familiar,
as though we'd been there once,
as though we all belonged there,
long, long ago,
before the last ice age,
in some primal place
before mills and industry,
before roads and rails.

                    -- Carol Mays

The Banquet

Divinity is to me
the connecting link,
the evolution of energy.
and love, likewise,
the dissolution of separation,
the current between gaps,
the transfusion of forces,
creativity unbounded.

Out for a stroll,
I am caught up in
three heavenly visions:
a white cloud passing,
a maple fluttering,
and a hornet exploring.
and these divine voices:
the chirping of a finch,
hammering in a yard,
the sound of someone's stereo.

In one common moment,
I am a communicant
in this feast of life—
its continuing burst
of expressions and ambitions,
its multifaceted forms.
Even the dancing Shiva
does not have the arms

to hold so much dear.

"Brother Sun; Sister Moon,"
This is joy undiluted—
we are each related
right to the core
down to the electrons
whizzing in us all.

			-- Carol Mays

Meditation

In the eye of many whirlwinds
Stays a deep, dark pool,
Tranquil and translucent,
At the vortex of Being,
Forever fed by subtle springs
Which give mysterious birth to
Thoughts pure and lucid
In their easy distillation.
Time is sure to transport, but
Mortality's ride is muffled
In this sweet, serene suspension.

-- Carol Mays

To Iris

Cooling, soothing, blue,
Delicate Lady
with understated frills,
sweet, yet bold,
starkly free,
growing wild near
reed and marsh:
In bygone eras,
perhaps one by your name,
sprang, like Athena,
from the forehead of Zeus.
For sometimes, now,
with penetrating purity
and Olympic skill,
you leap at will
through human eyes
to reclaim your origin
in the temple of the mind,
encircling the eye
as a rainbow, the sky,
garnishing our thoughts
with a pristine hope.

-- Carol Mays

Hidden Worlds

Some things I think are overhead
Are also underneath my bed
And this is true of you, as well.
So mark my words now, as I tell:
Beneath the clothing bins we store,
Under the stairs and basement floor,
Beneath the tracks of snails and slugs,
The homes of chipmunks, moles, and bugs,
Beneath the cracks where waters run
Through garnet and magnesium,
Below the mantle—an iron core,
More mantle, crust, then ocean floor,
With thermal vents, volcanic glint,
Turtles, whales, and tiny shrimp,
Beneath the driving winds and rain,
We find the stratosphere again.
And deeper still, the moon's bright face,
Then stars and wonders strewn through
    space.
So maybe now my claim is clear;
We rest upon a little sphere, and
"Up" and "Down" make sense alone
To Beings who are stuck at home.

-- Carol Mays

A Violet for Shiva

In a dim, desolate bog,
between the wavering shadows,
a violet shows its clear blue face
to the wan, desultory sun—
a sweet, pristine reminder
of perennial rotations—
rebirth, dissolution,
waxing from the waning;
all haunting and sublime.

-- Carol Mays

The Valley of Living
(song lyrics)

In the valley of life amid the mystical mountains,
We follow the pathway; we drink from the fountain.
We look to the stars for the clues they are giving, in the
    valley of living.

We are all on a journey, though we don't know where
    we're bound.
We don't know we are lost, but we want to be found.
We may stumble blindly as we journey through the
    night,
Never thinking to rest until it is light.

In the valley of life amid the mystical mountains,
We follow the pathway; we drink from the fountain.
We look to the stars for the clues they are giving, in the
    valley of living.

Where the journey started, we may never know,
and we may not conceive just where it will go.
Perhaps the destination is really not the goal.
Perhaps the path we're on is the path of the soul.

In the valley of life amid the mystical mountains,
We follow the pathway; we drink from the fountain.
We look to the stars for the clues they are giving in the
    valley of living.

-- Gary Blanchard

55

Heavenly Fire
(song lyrics)

We are children of the universe, beings filled with light.
We have all the answers as we journey to the height.
We have lived in majesty since the beginning of desire.
We are filled with heavenly fire.

We are made of stardust; we have moonbeams in our
  soul.
We can sail beyond the stars with the light that makes
  us whole.
We can reach the majesty to which we all aspire.
We are filled with heavenly fire.

We are filled with energy of a million-year-old force.
We are part of the galaxy, of the never-ending source.
Our heart is floating upward, our soul is rising higher.
We are filled with heavenly fire.

-- Gary Blanchard

In the Beginning . . .

A light has always been glowing
Close to the heart of the universe.
Over the course of time and evolution,
We as mortals have lived in fragile
   transience.
Yet flickering in the soul
Is the sublime, primordial sparkle.
In this ember born of the primal fire,
The transient contains the immortal
And the infinite caresses the finite.
Through the morass of earthly chaos,
The crystal beacon shines, and
Its power has not been extinguished.

-- Carol Mays

The Creator

He learned that God created the
    elephant and the oak
before he saw her run with the
    white-tailed deer
and paint the periwinkles.

They said the Creator reigned
    from a heavy helm
as he watched her bathing the
    moss of the pier
and kissing the boulder's crevices.

As they are no longer crude, they
    worship God as "One,"
but he feels her lighting on a
    swallowtail's wing
and shooting from sun to sun.

                    -- Carol Mays

Creation

Possibilities
glistening with energy
latency blooming

   -- Carol Mays

Selections from the Tao Te Ching

Before the birth of heaven and earth,
there was something infinite and inexhaustible,
self-possessed and pervasive—
the mother of all.
It cannot be named, but I call it, "Tao" ("The
    Way").
Though hardly perceivable,
 it continually inspires awe.
 Like the great rivers and seas,
 it ultimately flows through all things,
 softening that which is unyielding.
 If those in power could be centered in the Tao,
 the people would naturally defer to them,
 and peace would grace the earth
 like the sweet morning dew,
 which rests on everything equally.
 The risks of extremes would be avoided.

-- selections from the *Tao Te Ching*—
Attributed to Lao-Tzu (adapted from
several English translations)

Mystery Too
(song lyrics)

From the inner sense of time comes the
    ancient poet's rhyme.
Bringing us the master key to open up the
    mystery.

From the depth of time and space we arrive in
    quiet grace.
Finding what is meant to be as we explore the
    mystery.

Pouring forth from days gone by, we can hear
    the poet sigh.
From the depth of ecstasy, moving into
    mystery.

-- Gary Blanchard

"I, O Prince, am the Spirit which is well-seated in the consciousness of all beings, the reflection of which they each know as 'I," or the Ego. I am the Self that dwells in the heart of every mortal creature: I am the beginning, the life span, and the end of all.

I am the radiant sun among the light-givers: I am the mind; I am consciousness in the living.

I am death that snatches all; I, also, am the source of all that shall be born.

I am time without end: I am the sustainer; my face is everywhere. I am the beginning, the middle, and the end in creation:

I am the knowledge of things spiritual . . .
I am the divine seed of all lives. In this world nothing animate or inanimate exists without me . . . There is no limit to my divine manifestations.

Whatever in this world is powerful, beautiful, or glorious, that you may know to have come forth from a fraction of my power and glory."

-- from the Bhagavad-Gita

A Garden Beyond Paradise

Everything you see has its roots
   in the unseen world.
The forms may change,
   yet the essence remains the same.

Every wondrous sight will vanish,
every sweet word will fade.
   But do not be disheartened
The Source they come from is eternal—
growing, branching out,
   giving new life and new joy.

Why do you weep?—
That Source is within you,
 and this whole world
   is springing up from it.

The Source is full,
 its waters are ever-flowing;
   Do not grieve,
   drink your fill!
 Don't think it will ever run dry—
This is the endless Ocean! . . .

-- Jelaluddin Rumi,
-- Edited by Peter Y. Chou

The Deeper Dimension

Beneath the busy theater,
a little trap door,
modest and illusive,
opens to a space
infinite and peaceful—
a broader dimension,
resonant and real—
the silent birthing chamber
of all possibilities,
including, by surprise,
the gears animating
the action on the set.
One may find the door
and bask in this continuum
by stepping out of character
and shrugging off one's script,
releasing and recasting
preconceived props.

-- Carol Mays

Selection from the Chandogya Upanishad

In the center of the castle of Brahman, our own
    body,
there is a small shrine in the form of a lotus
    flower,
 and within can be found a small space.
 We should find who dwells there, and we
        should want to know him.

And if anyone asks, "Who is he who dwells in a
        small shrine in the center of the castle of
        Brahman?
Whom should we want to find and to know?"
    we can answer:

"The little space within the heart is as great as
        this vast universe.
The heavens and the earth are there, and the
        sun, and the moon, and the stars;
fire and lightning and winds are there;
    and all that now is and all that is not:
for the whole universe is in Him and He dwells
    within our heart."

                    -- from the Chandogya Upanishad,
                        -- Translated by Juan Mascaro
                        -- Reformatted by Carol Mays

Golden Thread

(song lyrics)

There is a golden thread that binds all of us in heart
    and mind
showing us that we can find the golden thread within.

The thread encloses many lands, it can be found in
    many strands.
It is thin and yet stands through all the threads of time.

The golden thread, as you will see, reaches out to you
    and me.
to make us as we ought to be, altogether whole.

Love your neighbor, try to do what you would want
    done to you.
Grab the thread and pull it through the fabric of your
    heart.

There is a golden thread that binds all of us in heart
    and mind.
showing us that we can find the golden thread within.

-- Gary Blanchard

Yin and Yang
(song lyrics)

Circle in a circle
Wheel within a wheel
Take a look inside you
Discover how you feel
Life is just a circle
No beginning and no end
Sometimes the circle's downward
Only to ascend
Since the world began
It's all inside the Yin and Yang.

Opposites attracting
Blending into one
Daytime turns to nighttime
The moon into the sun
Lightness and the darkness
Female and the male
Neither one descending
No one to prevail
Since the world began
It's all inside the Yin and Yang.

Sitting in the silence
Listen to the breeze
Flowing across the water
Ruffling the trees
Looking into nothing

To see what can be found
And while we are looking
The circle comes around
Since the world began
It's all inside the Yin and Yang.

    -- Gary Blanchard

III

Maritime Charm

The Sea of Sunset

This is the land the sunset washes,
These are the banks of the Yellow Sea;
Where it rose, or whither it rushes,
These are the western mystery!

Night after night her purple traffic
Strews the landing with opal bales;
Merchantmen poise upon horizons,
Dip, and vanish with fairy sails.

-- Emily Dickinson

The Lanterns of St. Eulalie

In the October afternoon
Orange and purple and maroon,

Goes quiet Autumn, lamp in hand,
About the apple-colored land,

To light in every apple-tree
The Lanterns of St. Eulalie.

They glimmer in the orchard shade
Like fiery opals set in jade,—

Crimson and russet and raw gold,
Yellow and green and scarlet old.

And O when I am far away
By foaming reef or azure bay,

In crowded street or hot lagoon,
Or under the strange austral moon,—

When the homesickness comes to me
For the great marshes by the sea,

The running dikes, the brimming tide,
And the dark firs on Fundy side,

In dreams once more I shall behold,

Like signal lights, those globes of gold

Hung out in every apple-tree—
The Lanterns of St. Eulalie.

-- Bliss Carman

Trade Winds

In the harbour, in the island, in the Spanish Seas,
Are the tiny white houses and the orange trees,
And day-long, night-long, the cool and pleasant
    breeze
Of the steady Trade Winds blowing.

There is the red wine, the nutty Spanish ale,
The shuffle of the dancers, the old salt's tale,
The squeaking fiddle, and the soughing in the sail
Of the steady Trade Winds blowing.

And o' nights there's fire-flies and the yellow moon,
And in the ghostly palm-trees the sleepy tune
Of the quiet voice calling me, the long low croon
Of the steady Trade Winds blowing.

-- John Masefield

Meeting at Night

The gray sea and the long black land;
And the yellow half-moon large and low;
And the startled little waves that leap
In fiery ringlets from their sleep,
As I gain the cove with pushing prow,
And quench its speed i' the slushy sand.

Then a mile of warm sea-scented beach;
Three fields to cross till a farm appears;
A tap at the pane, the quick sharp scratch
And blue spurt of a lighted match,
And a voice less loud, through its joys and
  fears,
Than the two hearts beating each to each!

-- Robert Browning

Night

A pale enchanted moon is sinking low
Behind the dunes that fringe the shadowy lea,
And there is haunted starlight on the flow
Of immemorial sea.

I am alone and need no more pretend
Laughter or smile to hide a hungry heart;
I walk with solitude as with a friend
Enfolded and apart.

We tread an eerie road across the moor
Where shadows weave upon their ghostly looms,
And winds sing an old lyric that might lure
Sad queens from ancient tombs.

I am a sister to the loveliness
Of cool far hill and long-remembered shore,
Finding in it a sweet forgetfulness
Of all that hurt before.

The world of day, its bitterness and cark,
No longer have the power to make me weep;
I welcome this communion of the dark
As toilers welcome sleep.

-- Lucy Maud Montgomery

The Golden City of St. Mary

Out beyond the sunset, could I but find the way,
Is a sleepy blue laguna which widens to a bay,
And there's the Blessed City -- so the sailors say --
    The Golden City of St. Mary.

It's built of fair marble -- white -- without a stain,
And in the cool twilight when the sea-winds wane
The bells chime faintly, like a soft, warm rain,
    In the Golden City of St. Mary.

Among the green palm-trees where the fire-flies
    shine,
Are the white tavern tables where the gallants dine,
Singing slow Spanish songs like old mulled wine,
    In the Golden City of St. Mary.

Oh I'll be shipping sunset-wards and westward-ho
Through the green toppling combers a-shattering
    into snow,
Till I come to quiet moorings and a watch below,
    In the Golden City of St. Mary.

-- John Masefield

The Sound of the Sea

The sea awoke at midnight from its sleep,
And round the pebbly beaches far and wide
I heard the first wave of the rising tide
Rush onward with uninterrupted sweep;
A voice out of the silence of the deep,
A sound mysteriously multiplied
As of a cataract from the mountain's side,
Or roar of winds upon a wooded steep.
So comes to us at times, from the unknown
And inaccessible solitudes of being,
The rushing of the sea-tides of the soul;
And inspirations, that we deem our own,
Are some divine foreshadowing and foreseeing
Of things beyond our reason or control.

-- Henry Wadsworth Longfellow

Exultation is the Going

Exultation is the going
Of an inland soul to sea,
Past the houses—past the headlands—
Into deep Eternity—

Bred as we, among the mountains,
Can the sailor understand
The divine intoxication
Of the first league out from land?

-- Emily Dickinson

The Sunken City

Hark! the faint bells of the sunken city
   Peal once more their wonted evening chime!
From the deep abysses floats a ditty,
   Wild and wondrous, of the olden time.

Temples, towers, and domes of many stories
   There lie buried in an ocean grave,--
Undescried, save when their golden glories
   Gleam, at sunset, through the lighted wave.

And the mariner who had seen them glisten,
   In whose ears those magic bells do sound,
Night by night bides there to watch and listen,
   Though death lurks behind each dark rock
     round.

So the bells of memory's wonder-city
   Peal for me their old melodious chime;
So my heart pours forth a changeful ditty,
   Sad and pleasant, from the bygone time.

Domes and towers and castles, fancy-builded,
   There lie lost to daylight's garish beams,--
There lie hidden till unveiled and gilded,
   Glory-gilded, by my nightly dreams!

And then hear I music sweet upknelling
   From many a well-known phantom band,

And, through tears, can see my natural
	dwelling
Far off in the spirit's luminous land!

					-- Wilhelm Mueller
		--Translation by James Clarence-Mangan

The Coral Grove

Deep in the wave is a coral grove,
Where the purple mullet, and gold-fish rove,
Where the sea-flower spreads its leave of blue,
That never are wet with falling dew,
But in bright and changeful beauty shine,
Far down in the green and glassy brine.
The floor is of sand, like the mountain drift,
And the pearl shells spangle the flinty snow;
From coral rocks the sea plants lift
Their boughs, where the tides and billows flow;
The water is calm and still below,
 For the winds and waves are absent there,
And the sands are bright as the stars that glow
 In the motionless fields of upper air . . .

-- James Gates Percival

IV

Fantastic Dreams

The Source of Magic

Magic in the mind
coming from the primal light
crystal refracted

Stardust and shadows
sweet fantasies unguarded
always transforming

-- Carol Mays

Calderon

(song lyrics)

Through the valley of Calderon,
Past the forest of Koh,
Over the mountains of Avalon,
There is a river that flows.
On the river there is a ship
That travels with the wind as it blows.

The ship sails east in the summer breeze
To the far-away land of Tarway.
The breeze runs free through the spreading tree,
Past the children at play.
The sun shines bright up until the night
Brings a sudden end of the day.

Where is the valley of Calderon?
Where is the forest of Koh?
Where is the place that the ship has gone?
Where is the river that flows?
Where are the children who play all day?
Is it a place that we can go?

Calderon is a state of mind; Koh a place in the soul.
The river flows through the sands of time
Where all the lost are made whole.
The children play in the magic day
When the bells of peace will be tolled.

                                   -- Gary Blanchard

A Glimpse

An image comes unbidden
in a quickening flash:
the dark silhouette of
a female, part avian,
upright and still
in a moss-clad marsh,
poised in the luster
of a golden half-sun.
The ongoing joy
of such fleeting thoughts:
a secret skylight
in a 10' by 12' room.

-- Carol Mays

Secrets in a Storm

Secrets sail on the whirling winds,
along with the dark and driven clouds.
Carried aloft with litter and leaves
are invisible, partly submerged longings:

to hitch a ride on the primal rawness,
to abandon all things set and tethered,
to project oneself toward the unknown,
while thriving through the natural chaos.

-- Carol Mays

Night-Flying

I drift aloft with gossamer wings,
slowly slanting toward the moon,
beaming with its nimbus glow.

Like me, it seems to shift positions,
darting between forms and shadows,
darkened slopes and rounded hills.

Shimmering streams grow mute below us,
sending clear, sweet twinkles skyward—
forever gracing souls in flight.

-- Carol Mays

Lunar Tune
(song lyrics)

Riding on a shooting star; heading out toward a
   dream,
tomorrow's even closer than it seems.

Moving through the cloudless sky; heading out
    toward the moon,
I am dancing to the lunar tune.

Life goes by so quickly and time just slips away,
   but tomorrow brings a brighter day.

Soaring out among the planets, in the vast array
    of space;
I can feel the moon's embrace.

Life goes by so quickly and time just slips away,
   but tomorrow brings a brighter day.

Riding on a shooting star, heading out toward a
   dream;
tomorrow's even closer than it seems.

-- Gary Blanchard

An Archetype

Somewhere in an old-growth forest,
a woman smoothly moves amidst
shadows of the pines and hardwoods.
Her mossy gown is verdant green,
her hair twinkles with mica, and
her soul, deep as a midnight sky,
with remote star clusters beaming.
She tends the ruins of an ancient inn
and a bed of ferns and roses.
Many a nomad, passing through,
is revived by her grace and goodness.
Though we can't lay hands on her,
she wanders free within our grasp,
For the ancient inn beguiles us still
in the labyrinths of our minds.

-- Carol Mays

The Song of the Wandering Aengus

I went out to the hazel wood,
Because a fire was in my head,
And cut and peeled a hazel wand,
And hooked a berry to a thread;
And when white moths were on the wing,
And moth-like stars were flickering out,
I dropped the berry in a stream
And caught a little silver trout.

When I had laid it on the floor
I went to blow the fire a-flame,
But something rustled on the floor,
And someone called me by my name:
It had become a glimmering girl
With apple blossom in her hair
Who called me by my name and ran
And faded through the brightening air.

Though I am old with wandering
Through hollow lands and hilly lands,
I will find out where she has gone,
And kiss her lips and take her hands;
And walk among long dappled grass,
And pluck till time and times are done,
The silver apples of the moon,
The golden apples of the sun.

-- William Butler Yeats

The Siesta

The sky was yellow, with sparkling beams
in iridescent gold
reflected on the pointed hat
of an elf, two centuries old.

The hostess of the hour was sweet
in a robe of mismatched dyes.
She entertained with merely this—
a kiss in her root beer eyes.

The placemats were of baby fern,
woven in intricate green,
and laughter was heard
like the tinkling of bells
near the banks of an ebony stream.

I boarded a raft for an underground cave,
which was carved in a spiral pattern.
The subterranean symphony hall
was draped in coral satin.

At the end of the course, was a waterslide
in hues of ultraviolet,
with children bouncing up and down.
They prevailed upon me to try it.

Though some might want to interpret this,
myself, I'm in no hurry

93

to analyze such a sweet retreat
which woke me without a worry.

                    -- Carol Mays

Fairyland

Leprechauns and elves
leaping through the synapses
of our minds' playgrounds.

-- Carol Mays

The Eyes of Enchantment

Magic loves the indistinct,
clandestine and obscure.

The eerie reflections
of twinkling jack-o'-lanterns
deepen in darkness . . .

Refracted lights on fir trees
multiply patterns . . .

Landscapes concealed in snow
hint at other worlds . . .

Shrouded lakes exhaling mist . . .
amorphous nighttime shadows . . .
secret codes and quests . . .
romantic dreams and visions . . .
a bride's veiled countenance . . .

Vagueness makes room
for new possibilities.
We yearn for something more
than 20/20 vision.

-- Carol Mays

Wild Winged Ones

Sophisticated ladies,
embellished by eons,
illusive, enchanting,
with black velvet "eyes,"
and fringed yellow cloaks,
sparkling with diamonds
at midnight and dawn,
Oh, fly me away from
my grey-flooded days,
from the four-lane race
and the file drawer maze.
Fly me away from
the chain of the clock
and the sink of necessities.
Bring me in spirit
to magical rendezvous,
to dance by the glint
of the moon on the marsh,
hiding from fireflies,
nudging antennas.

-- Carol Mays

I Heard the Mermaids Singing
(song lyrics)

I heard the mermaids singing,
listened to their siren song,
over the seas their voices ringing,
calling me to come along.

There's magic in the music,
and it dances in my soul.
I feel my heart is ringing,
and my spirit is made whole.

I heard the mermaids singing
from their home along the shore,
telling of the life they're living,
showing me that there is more.

As I wonder at their beauty,
I can feel my spirit soar.
I feel a peace and pleasure
that is magic to explore.

I heard the mermaids singing,
listened to their siren song,
over the seas their voices ringing,
calling me to come along.

There's magic in the music,
and it dances in my soul.

I feel my heart is ringing,
and my spirit is made whole.

        -- Gary Blanchard

Amphibians

When life is losing its meaning,
And the glorious colors grow pale,
And death seems the one destination,
Remember the humble toad,
Doomed to spend drier days
Digging deep in the arid ground,
Seeking survival and shelter,
But to be loving and birthing,
It later returns to the flow
Of a resilient milieu that bestows
The clarity of radiant expanse
And the nudges of buoyant kin.

Perhaps the insular, dreary days
Are partly an illusion
And existence points not to the grave,
But to a metamorphosis,
In which we shed these calloused feet
And bathe in the nurturing nexus
Of our birth-home, the sea.

-- Carol Mays

Fantasies

Somewhere,
music is eternal and dance is the soul unleashed.
Emanating from bird nests,
melodies rise with the sun and stars.
Cellos call from sand dunes and seas.

Somewhere,
sparkling-haired children in yellow silk,
sprinkled with sun rays,
dance with no audience on a hill,
amidst the scent of lilacs, earth, and sun.

Somewhere,
blue, green, and purple mist mingle at evening,
when roses grow without thorns,
and women in glowing robes walk near streams
of snow landing as natural lace.

-- Carol Mays

Sea Sunset

. . . A city of the Land of Lost Delight,
On seas enchanted,
Presently to be lost in mist moon-white
And music-haunted;
Given but briefly to our raptured vision,
With all its opal towers and shrines elysian.

Had we some mystic boat with pearly oar
And wizard pilot,
To guide us safely by the siren shore
And cloudy islet,
We might embark and reach that shining portal
Beyond which linger dreams and joys immortal.

But we may only gaze with longing eyes
On those far, sparkling
Palaces in the fairy-peopled skies,
O'er waters darkling,
Until the winds of night come shoreward roaming,
And the dim west has only gray and gloaming.

-- Lucy Maud Montgomery

At the Library

Pure possibility plays
among the shorter shelves.
Here can be quickly glanced,
quite easily, per chance:
glittering, spinning castles
with multi-colored shrubs;
space-suited clowns
juggling throwing stars;
a grinning seahorse bobbing
weightless in thin air;
alleys winding dark and light,
with neon-green monsters;
kindly whlte-haired grandpas
speaking distant dialects.

-- Carol Mays

Bunny Buzz

Sweet Easter candies
buried in shredded grasses.
Magic hides all night.

-- Carol Mays

Black Magic

Soft as mist,
slowly advancing
in shadowy silence,
sure-footed, steady, she
searches me with steadfast eyes,
sparked, it seems, by latent lightning,
smoldering still with sultry enchantment,
she stealthily leaps now to my lap, sitting
sweetly, safeguarding unfathomable secrets.

-- Carol Mays

To a Raven

Fearless Raven, soaring in
the rich, dark chasm—
that world of shadows, echoes,
cliffs and crags chaotic,
the void of subtle stirrings in
a quintessential midnight—
Make some room for me
on your old, straight wings.
I, too, need to sense
lightning piercing stardust,
galvanizing mountains,
stoking distant thunder.
Let me catch a breath
of your pure, primeval air,
exotic and unshackling
latent, raw, unbounded.

--Carol Mays

Beacons

The eyes of heavenly beacons
Peek out from amidst the shadows,
Like so many playful stars
Behind a mist-blown sky—
Or the diffuse glow of street lamps
Draped with sculpted snow.
From songbirds to sonatas,
From meteors to mantras,
They veil themselves in fetching garb
And wink at us as a lover.

-- Carol Mays

Insanity

I saw the little old man
with long white hair and yellow eyes
whisking on windy nights
through street lights and puddles.
I told him how I spend twelve hours a day,
chasing, racing, and bracing,
and he gave me a wink and a yawn.
I asked him how I could stay awhile
on his sweet, secret, gentle side,
but he vanished without a clue.

-- Carol Mays

The Earth-Spirit

Down these golden uplands, I
Move with sunny winds and sky,
Where the ghosts of waters are,
To the gates of dusk and star.

And I know that as I go,
She whose bosom is the snow
Of the birch and aspen tree,
Dreams these sunny dreams with me.

She whose glance and gleam of hair
Are the ruddy spinning, rare,
Of the gold glint of the sun
In the wood when day is done;

She whose inner speech is heard
In the hush of wind and bird,
And whose soul is as a star
Cradled where the hill-lakes are.

-- Wilfred Campbell

An April Night

. . . Down on the marshlands with flicker and
  glow
Wanders Will-o'-the-Wisp through the night,
Seeking for witch-gold lost long ago
By the glimmer of goblin lantern-light.

The night is a sorceress, dusk-eyed and
  dear,
Akin to all eerie and elfin things,
Who weaves about us in meadow and mere
The spell of a hundred vanished Springs.

-- Lucy Maud Montgomery

V

Alluring Hauntings

October 30

Vague intimations
mist and spirits coalesce--
pleasant harbingers

-- Carol Mays

October Fest

Homes so recently abandoned
for Sunday swims and picnics
Have become indoor respites
from the restless chill of change.

Secure, still days have vanished
with hazy meadows humming.
Fireflies have met their end,
replaced with jack-o'-lanterns.

Now forewarning breezes,
stealthy, crisp, and vibrant
Pierce preoccupations,
uncovering reckless impulses.

Now uncanny images,
voices of chance and charm,
Bide their ghostly time
to tease mortals hitherto content.

Darts and dashes of circumstance,
figures of flitting moments,
Are creatures mysteriously born,
skipping towards certain death.

So what, if the end is approaching;
the witches' brew is bubbling—
The whispers of all moans and laughs,

the collage of dreams and desires.

Now is the ecstasy of flinging
one's fate to the unrefined choir—
The discordant sounds and initiatives
of many spirits and springs.

Grinning gourds and goblins
bless this annual surprise—
This primal burst of forces
that refuse once more to be quenched.

-- Carol Mays

A Magical Halloween Pin

As Halloween approached,
a middle-age redhead,
working in a coffee shop,
boldly wore a spider pin.
It had a massive body
of ruby-colored glass,
and was, in subdued lighting,
as striking as her smile.
In that one adornment
of child-like abandon,
she loaned me a key
to a fluid dimension—
a sweet, hidden wellspring,
expansive, when tapped,
of all possibilities,
where young may be old,
and old may be young
where in the mortal struggle
against prosaic prudence
and tired perspectives,
bewitchment can prevail—
a phoenix from ashes—
in magical resiliency,
wondrous, warm, and winking.

-- Carol Mays

The Pumpkin
(fourth stanza)

. . . Oh, fruit loved of boyhood! the old days
   recalling,
When wood-grapes were purpling and brown
   nuts were falling!
When wild, ugly faces we carved in its skin,
Glaring out through the dark with a candle
   within!
When we laughed round the corn-heap, with
   hearts all in tune,
Our chair a broad pumpkin,—our lantern the
   moon,
Telling tales of the fairy who travelled like steam,
In a pumpkin-shell coach, with two rats for her
   team! . . .

-- John Greenleaf Whittier

Trick-or-Treating

The sweet-sour scent of waning hay
    drifts to town from nearby fields,
    pleasing all walkers with an edgy peace.

While autumn gusts enliven shadows,
    the wavering moon turns sheets to ghosts,
    and disguises reveal diverse fancies.

The mind evokes bewitching specters
    cavorting like bats on their nightly hunts,
    quickening the pace of parent and child.

Spooky music beckons from porches,
    conjuring up faux frights and terrors,
    as diffuse mysteries tug at innocence.

                    -- Carol Mays

Ulalume—A Ballad

The skies they were ashen and sober;
    The leaves they were crisped and sere—
    The leaves they were withering and sere;
It was night in the lonesome October
    Of my most immemorial year:
It was hard by the dim lake of Auber,
    In the misty mid region of Weir—
It was down by the dank tarn of Auber,
    In the ghoul-haunted woodland of Weir.

Here once, through an alley Titanic,
    Of cypress, I roamed with my Soul—
    Of cypress, with Psyche, my Soul.
These were days when my heart was volcanic
    As the scoriac rivers that roll—
    As the lavas that restlessly roll
Their sulphurous currents down Yaanek,
    In the ultimate climes of the Pole—
That groan as they roll down Mount Yaanek,
    In the realms of the Boreal Pole.

Our talk had been serious and sober,
    But our thoughts they were palsied and
        sere—
    Our memories were treacherous and sere;

    For we knew not the month was October,
        And we marked not the night of the year—

(Ah, night of all nights in the year!)
We noted not the dim lake of Auber,
    (Though once we had journeyed down here)--
We remembered not the dank tarn of Auber,
    Nor the ghoul-haunted woodland of Weir.

And now, as the night was senescent,
    And the star-dials pointed to morn—
    As the star-dials hinted of morn—
At the end of our path a liquescent
    And nebulous lustre was born,
Out of which a miraculous crescent
    Arose with a duplicate horn—
Astarte's bediamonded crescent,
    Distinct with its duplicate horn.
And I said—"She is warmer than Dian:
    She rolls through an ether of sighs—
    She revels in a region of sighs.

She has seen that the tears are not dry on
    These cheeks, where the worm never dies,
And has come past the stars of the Lion,
    To point us the path to the skies—
    To the Lethean peace of the skies—
Come up, in despite of the Lion,
    To shine on us with her bright eyes—
Come up, through the lair of the Lion,
    With love in her luminous eyes."

But Psyche, uplifting her finger,

Said—"Sadly this star I mistrust—
  Her pallor I strangely mistrust—
Ah, hasten!—ah, let us not linger!
  Ah, fly!—let us fly!—for we must."
In terror she spoke; letting sink her
  Wings till they trailed in the dust—
In agony sobbed; letting sink her
  Plumes till they trailed in the dust—
  Till they sorrowfully trailed in the dust.

I replied—"This is nothing but dreaming.
  Let us on, by this tremulous light!
  Let us bathe in this crystalline light!
Its Sibylic splendor is beaming
  WIth Hope and in Beauty to-night—
  See!—it flickers up the sky through the night!
Ah, we safely may trust to its gleaming
  And be sure it will lead us aright—
We surely may trust to a gleaming
  That cannot but guide us aright,
Since it flickers up to Heaven through the
  night."

Thus I pacified Psyche and kissed her,
  And tempted her out of her gloom—
  And conquered her scruples and gloom;
And we passed to the end of the vista—
  But were stopped by the door of a tomb—
  By the door of a legended tomb;
And I said: "What is written, sweet sister,

On the door of this legended tomb?"
She replied—"Ulalume—Ulalume!—
'Tis the vault of thy lost Ulalume!"

Then my heart it grew ashen and sober
   As the leaves that were crisped and sere—
   As the leaves that were withering and sere—
And I cried: "It was surely October,
   On *this* very night of last year,
   That I journeyed—I journeyed down here!—
   That I brought a dread burden down here—
   On this night, of all nights in the year,
   Ah, what demon hath tempted me here?
Well I know, now, this dim lake of Auber—
   This misty mid region of Weir:--
Well I know, now, this dank tarn of Auber—
   This ghoul-haunted woodland of Weir."

Said we, then—the two, then—"Ah, can it
   Have been that the woodlandish ghouls—
   The pitiful, the merciful ghouls,
To bar up our way and to ban it
   From the secret that lies in these wolds—
   From the thing that lies hidden in these wolds--
Have drawn up the spectre of a planet
   From the limbo of lunary souls—
This sinfully scintillant planet
   From the Hell of the planetary souls?"

               -- Edgar Allan Poe

The Lake of the Dismal Swamp

"They made her a grave, too cold and damp
For a soul so warm and true;
And she's gone to the Lake of the Dismal Swamp,
Where, all night long, by a fire-fly lamp,
She paddles her white canoe.

And her fire-fly lamp I soon shall see,
And her paddle I soon shall hear;
Long and loving our life shall be,
And I'll hide the maid in a cypress tree,
When the footstep of death is near."

Away to the Dismal Swamp he speeds—
His path was rugged and sore,
Through tangled juniper, beds of reeds,
Through many a fen where the serpent feeds,
And man never trod before.

And when on the earth he sunk to sleep,
If slumber his eyelids knew,
He lay where the deadly vine doth weep
Its venomous tear and nightly steep
The flesh with blistering dew!

And near him the she-wolf stirr'd the brake,
And the copper-snake breath'd in his ear,
TIll he starting cried, from his dream awake,
"Oh! when shall I see the dusky Lake,

And the white canoe of my dear?"

He saw the Lake, and a meteor bright
Quick over its surface play'd—
"Welcome," he said, "my dear one's light!"
And the dim shore echoed for many a night
The name of the death-cold maid.

Till he hollow'd a boat of the birchen bark,
Which carried him off from shore;
Far, far he follow'd the meteor spark,
The wind was high and the clouds were dark,
And the boat return'd no more.

But oft, from the Indian hunter's camp,
This lover and maid so true
Are seen at the hour of midnight damp
To cross the Lake by a fire-fly lamp,
And paddle their white canoe!

-- Thomas Moore

Halloween Twilight

In the shifting air,
the sweet scent of candy corn,
candle wax burning.

All doors are open.
an ancient mystery lives.
I bask in its glow.

-- Carol Mays

VI

Unexpected Treasures

A Toast

To butterflies, bats, and midnight creatures,
To the brilliant, the dark, and things unseen.
To the secret allure of ultraviolet,
To a lucid child-like dream.

To the musty scent of ancient places,
To thoughts distilled on a fragile page,
To open-ended expectations, and
Eccentricities of a secret sage.

To the promise that lies in what is unfinished,
To the charm in the rawness of the fray,
To quests that lead to curious changes,
And rest that unbinds peace and play.

-- Carol Mays

Luminescence

Dazzling wind-blown light
sprinkles a wavy surface
with meandering beacons,
offering to the passerby
seeds of sprite-like joy.
The sunlit sparkles shift
according to perspective,
aligning with the angle—
sun to lake to eyes:
Angels in the angles—
a trajectory of dreams.

-- Carol Mays

Bewitching Distant Landscape

The treetops rustle and quiver
as though at this hour
about the ruined walls
the ancient gods were making their rounds.

Here beyond the myrtle trees
in the quiet shimmer of twilight,
what are you telling me, confused as in
   dreams,
fantastic night?

The stars all shine upon me
with the glow of love;
the far horizon speaks ecstatically
as if of great happiness to come.

                    -- Joseph Eichendorff
                    --Translated by Philip L. Miller

Home

I found in the woods
a sweet women's getaway—
a warm place of peace.

Covered with ivy,
a stone cottage connected
to earth and to sky.

-- Carol Mays

Vapor and Blue

Domed with the azure of heaven,
Floored with a pavement of pearl,
Clothed all about with a brightness
Soft as the eyes of a girl,

Girt with a magical girdle,
Rimmed with a vapor of rest—
These are the inland waters,
These are the lakes of the west.

Voices of slumberous music,
Spirits of mist and of flame,
Moonlit memories left here
By gods who long ago came,

And vanishing left but an echo
In silence of moon-dim caves,
Where haze-wrapt the August night slumbers,
Or the wild heart of October raves.

Here where the jewels of nature
Are set in the light of God's smile,
Far from the world's wild throbbing,
I will stay me and rest me awhile.

And store in my heart old music,
Melodies gathered and sung

By the genies of love and of beauty
When the heart of the world was young.

-- William Wilfred Campbell

From a Child

Something's wild in the woods tonight—
Something crisp in the breeze.
There's some sweet scent in the shadows.
Hundreds of creatures, hiding out
with eyes and ears wide open.
It seems to me that the forest itself,
young and true, yet ages old,
Is hovering here and everywhere
in a long, black, sparkling cloak.

                              -- Carol Mays

The Children's Entrance

To children's eyes in mid-December,
a city street winks and twinkles.
The towering collage of lights and patterns
seems majestic and surreal.
Silvers, reds, and living greens
all conjure up exotic scents and
whisper hints of private promises,
smiling, shining, blowing kisses.

-- Carol Mays

Block Party

Dance, Ladies, dance!—
By the light of lanterns.
Let your red skirts swirl
Like the tops of carousels—
Candy-apple red.

Dance, Children, dance!
With your glowing adornments—
Rainbow blue and green—
Firefly green.

The scent of gardenias
Wafts from urban gardens—
Gardenias and radishes.
The night air breathes magic;
The block has been transformed.

-- Carol Mays

Crossways

Summer night pulsing
Streak of jets landing
Sapphire lights winking

Minds ricocheting
Lovers embracing
Cologne, silk caressing

Muscle maneuvering
Luggage uplifting
Strength celebrating

Interstate soaring
Windows, dash, dancing
Jazz and soul rocking

Frequency sampling
Circuits infusing
Earth-force vibrating.

-- Carol Mays

Newport at Night

City lights sparkling,
mirrored in the Bay,
multi-colored jewels—
amber, rose, and green,
crystal, diamond-white—
gracing bridge and buildings—
mansions, pubs, and shops—
fanciful reflections of
countless points of intrigue.
Neurons, lives entwining—
schemes, ideas, and passions—
complex as a motherboard,
vibrant as a heartbeat,
fertile and entrancing,
as though fashioned by a
cosmic magician's spell.

-- Carol Mays

Flint

An emerald is as green as grass,
   A ruby red as blood;
A sapphire shines as blue as heaven;
   A flint lies in the mud.

A diamond is a brilliant stone,
   To catch the world's desire;
An opal holds a fiery spark;
   But a flint holds fire.

-- Christina Rossetti

To Mozart

Upon hearing what you heard
And relayed with such devotion,
The soul arises as a bird from a puddle,
Shaking off its present absorptions,
Abandoning its own reflection,
Drawn toward an infinite horizon,
It's nudged along by wind-borne petals,
Entranced by a piercing blue
In a sheer, receptive sky.

-- Carol Mays

Epiphany

Some time ago, on a somber day,
I suddenly sensed a channel
through which I could swim to the sea—
the grand, radiant, infinite sea,
promising purpose and pleasure
and brimming with love and life.

Pedestrian pebbles and roiling rain
now threaten to flood the entrance,
eroding this bright epiphany,
but I have mapped the sacred site,
and my fins, stored and suspended,
are starting to bend unbidden.

-- Carol Mays

Cross-Reference for Music and Videos

Carol Mays has created multimedia presentations of many of the poems in this book. They may be viewed on YouTube, by going to www.youtube.com/user/IdyllicProductions.

To hear and download Gary Blanchard's songs or see his videos, go to www.garyblanchardmusic.com. Alternatively, a song may be available, if you ask your Amazon, Google, or Apple device to play it.

"Heart of the Sun" – *Journey of Life* CD.

"Peace Like a River" – *Journey of Life* CD.

"Hands of Time"—*From an upcoming* CD.

"Calderon"—*Journey of Life* CD.

"Lunar Tune" -- *To a Dreamer* CD.

"Heavenly Fire" – *The Inner Light* CD

"The Valley of Living" – *The Inner Light* CD

"Yin and Yang" – *Professor Sorghum's Clockwork Apothecary* CD

"At Perception's Edge" – *Children of the Sun* CD

"I Heard the Mermaids Singing" – *Light One Candle*
   CD

"Golden Thread" – *Light One Candle* CD

"Mystery Too" – *Light One Candle* CD

Bibliography

Much of the public domain poetry reprinted in this book was originally obtained from multiple on-line poetry sites; however, the reader may find the following references helpful.

Campbell, William Wilfred. *Selected Poetry and Essays.* Ontario, Canada: Wilfrid Laurier University Press, 1987.

Campbell, Wilfred. *The Poems of Wilfred Campbell.* Toronto, Canada: William Briggs, *1905*

Carman, Bliss. *The World's Best Poetry.* Great Neck, N.Y.: Granger Book Company, Inc., 1981

Carman, Bliss and Hovey, Richard. *Last Songs from Vagabondia.* Boston, MA: Forgotten Books, 2012. Originally Published 1900.

Ferns, John and McCabe, Kevin. *The Poetry of Lucy Maud Montgomery.* Canada: Fitzhenry & Whiteside, 1999

Hollander, John, Compiler. *American Poetry: The Nineteenth Century,* Volumes I and II. New York, N.Y.: Penguin Books, 1993.

Johnson, Thomas, Editor. *The Complete Poems of Emily Dickinson*. Boston, MA: Little, Brown and Company, 1960.

Kilcup, Karen and Sorby, Angela, Editors. *Over the River and Through the Woods; An Anthology of Nineteenth Century American Children's Poetry*. Baltimore, Maryland: The Johns Hopkins University Press, 2014.

Mascaro, Juan. *The Upanishads; Translations from the Sanskrit*. New York, New York: Penguin Putnam, 1965.

Masefield, John. *Salt-Water Poems and Ballads*. New York, N.Y.: The MacMillan Company Publishers, 1914.

Masefield, John. *Spunyarn; Sea Poetry and Prose*. London, England: Penguin Group, 2011.

Masefield, John. *The Collected Poems*. London, England: William Heinemann LTD, 1923.
Mays, Carol. *Building a Faith for the Future*. North Charleston, South Carolina: Create Space Independent Publishing Platform, 2016.

Mays, Carol. *Halloween Enchantment; Haunting Poems and Stories*. North Charleston, South Carolina: Create Space Independent Publishing Platform, 2017.

Mays, Carol. *Poems of Peace and Renewal.* North Charleston, South Carolina: Create Space Independent Publishing Platform, 2012.

Mays, Carol. *Stardust, Shadows, and Secrets.* North Charleston, South Carolina: Create Space Independent Publishing Platform, 2014.

Mays, Carol Ann. *Strategies, Poems, and Stories for Holistic Living.* North Charleston, South Carolina: Create Space Independent Publishing Platform, 2010.

Mays, Carol. *The Mystique of the Sea; Poems, Stories, and Intriguing Facts.* West Brookfield, Massachusetts: Amazon, 2019.

Mays, Carol. *Uplifting Poems.* North Charleston, South Carolina: Create Space Independent Publishing Platform, 2016.

Mays, Carol; Bachtold, Richard; and Andersen, Nina. *Mystical Poems by Three Contemporary New England Writers.* North Charleston, South Carolina: Create Space Independent Publishing Platform, 2011.

Mays, Carol; Delaney, Suzanne. *Poems of Nature, Enchantment, and Mystery.* West Brookfield, Massachusetts: Amazon, 2020.

McClatchy, J.D., Editor. *Poems of the Sea*. New York, N.Y.: Alfred A. Knopf, 2001.

Miller, Philip. *The Ring of Words; An Anthology of Song Texts*. New York, New York: W.W. Norton & Company, 1963.

Opie, Iona and Opie, Peter--Editors. *The Oxford Book of Children's Verse*. New York, New York: Oxford University Press, 1973.

Rumi, Jelaluddin. *A Garden Beyond Paradise: The Mystical Poetry of Rumi* (translated by Jonathan Star). New York, New York: Bantam Books, 1992.

Solley, George C. and Steinbaugh, Eric. *Moods of the Sea*. Annapolis, Maryland: Naval Institute Press, 1981.

Yang, Wan-li. *Heaven My Blanket, Earth My Pillow* (translated by Jonathan Chaves). New York, New York: Weatherhill, 1975.

Other Works by Carol Mays:

Strategies, Poems, & Stories for Holistic Living—Three genres in one book, on the theme of avoiding some of society's subtle negative influences and living a fulfilling life.

Poems of Peace and Renewal—Poems from various sources on the themes of peace and renewal.

Halloween Stories & Games for Mixed-Age Parties—A short book that includes fanciful Halloween stories, with optional sound effects for audience participation.

Stardust, Shadows, and Secrets—Three genres in one book, on the theme of creating and enjoying intrigue and enchantment in life. It includes essays, poetry, and a novella about a young woman who finds a mysterious carnival in the woods behind her house and, through this discovery, ends up accidentally transforming her hometown.

Building a Faith for the Future—A serious, inspiring book that examines the pros and cons of various religions and some of the cultural factors which inhibit spiritual well-being. It presents a new approach to understanding and living one's faith.

Uplifting Poems—A beautiful and inspiring compilation of poems by many writers, including classical, on the subjects of Nature, Connection, Fantasy, Magic, Hope, and Play.

Halloween Enchantment; Haunting Poems and Stories—A collection of poems and stories for all who seek an eerie escape from the mundane.

The Mystique of the Sea; Poems, Stories, and Intriguing Facts—Carol combined and compiled three genres in one book to express in various forms the mystique of the sea.

Carol collaborated with Richard Bachtold and Nina Andersen on *Mystical Poems by Three Contemporary New England Writers*—a beautiful book of inspiring, moving poetry.

She collaborated with Suzanne Delaney on *Poems of Nature, Enchantment, and Mystery.* This is another book replete with lovely, magical images.

Poems of Enchantment—An unusual, enchanting, and relaxing DVD which includes poem narrations, visuals, music, and sound effects.

The above works are available from well-known, online sellers, as well as through local vendors.